A Consistent Life

The young advocate's guide to living peace and justice daily

Mary Grace Coltharp
& Aimee Murphy

Mary Grace Coltharp & Aimee Murphy

Contents

"The inherent dignity of humanity
is the foundation upon which all human rights lay.
Without this intrinsic human worth at the core of our philosophy,
all manner of unjust discrimination could be justified.
We are not valuable because of our age, race, size, religion, sexuality,
or even our innocence or usefulness:
we have immutable worth simply because we are human.
Support or tacit acceptance of any act of violence -
whether it be by abortion or by drones, by execution or by euthanasia
- undermines any of our work for human rights.

Either we all deserve to live without violence... or none of us do."
-Aimee Murphy

Mary Grace Coltharp & Aimee Murphy

Introduction

Welcome to the next year of your life, a year you have dedicated to life, peace, and justice. This book will be a source of information, a launch pad for inspiration and reflection, and a guide for you to put your passion into action. At times, the most difficult part of creating positive change is knowing what to do *today*, but now you have in your hands a guidebook. We've organized this so that each week you will:

- Learn a little about a topic related to the Consistent Life Ethic (CLE),
- Be called on to do further research,
- And have some ideas of actions you can take

in order to
create a more just, peaceful, and life-affirming culture.

Using this book:
- This was written for individuals but can easily be used by a club or a group of friends.
- The actions for each day are set up in groups of five, totaling 260 days, with the idea being that for each 7-day week in a year you have 5 days of tasks to use how you like.
- Each five day section focuses your attention on a particular group of human beings that face injustice and therefore need their dignity restored - they must be rehumanized.
- The last of each 5 day grouping is a challenge that requires more time and planning. I suggest that at the beginning of each week, or page of challenges, you read that last day's task, or even all five tasks.
- Each day includes a space for you to write the date on which you did or plan to complete it.

- If you are a student, school may be your full time job right now, but you can find a way to incorporate these issues into papers and other assignments you may get, blending your education and interest in social justice.
- I suggest keeping track of your volunteer hours for future scholarship opportunities and the like.
- Make these pages as interactive as possible. If a certain topic interests you or you really loved a particular challenge, then bookmark it so you can come back to it.
- The last topic and page of challenges we left open for you to fill with your own ideas. Throughout this year you'll come up with new and specific tasks. You can keep track of them all to try out in the future.
- If you come across an activity that you find difficult or out of your comfort zone, invite your friends and family to join you. Ease yourself into tasks that are stressful, and be patient with yourself. Every voice is needed in the effort for human rights.
- If there is something you don't think you are particularly skilled at, like art, writing, or talking about difficult issues, try it anyway. Before we really joined the pro-life movement, many of us had no idea we could be leaders, but because of our work as activists we've gained incalculable confidence.
- All the tasks we ask of you have been included for a reason. We suggest researching on your own because learning something for yourself will make it stick in your head better. Also, you'll be able to find the specific statistics or stories that will personally touch you and make the issue mean something more to you. There are self-care tasks to make sure you're not neglecting to rehumanize yourself either. The artistic challenges help work a different part of your brain and are important reminders that we aren't just *ending* injustice but we're also *creating* a better world.

The quotations presented in this booklet have been carefully chosen for the truth they illustrate. However, the originators of these quotes do not all necessarily fully represent the mission and vision of Rehumanize International. We recognize the thoughts shared through these quotes speak to the Consistent Life Ethic well, even if their speakers did not always speak or act in accordance with it.

A note from Mary Grace:

As the central author of this guidebook I would also like to speak to my perspective. I write about racial and economic injustice from the privileged point of view of a middle-class, white American teen. I bring up immigration but the Coltharp family has been here since before this land even became the United States of America. I speak out against the injustice and violence of abortion but I have never been pregnant and I don't recall my months as a fetus. I don't know what it's like to go to war any more than I know what it's like to live in a war torn region. I have less than a couple decades on this earth and no disabilities or terminal illnesses. Lastly, I've never been imprisoned, convicted, or even had a brush with the law. I tell you all this not to discredit myself, but to give you an honest context to what I've written. I wrote this book for you not because I've had much personal experience with human rights violations but because I *haven't*. As the author and Holocaust survivor, Elie Wiesel, said, "We must take sides. Neutrality helps the oppressor, never the victim. Silence encourages the tormentor, never the tormented." Whether you are a young activist like myself, or if you are decades older and wiser, I hope you will take this book as a call to action to be more than a bystander in this world aching for human rights, human dignity, and healing.

You will rehumanize every human being!

According to *merriam-webster.com* "dehumanize" is a verb defined as "to deprive of human qualities, personality, or spirit"[1], but you are not powerless to the dehumanization that can be so rampant in our world! You can...

Rehumanize

verb. /rē'(h)yōōmə nīz/

1. To restore to humans the sense of selfhood and individuality
2. To recognize and respect the inherent dignity due to human beings after they have been dehumanized

RehumanizeIntl.org

First you must examine your own relationships with other human beings. Friends and family probably come to mind first, but think beyond them until you get to the human beings you pass on the street, classmates you've never spoken to, your Uber driver or neighbor. Who in your life do you ignore? Who gets ignored by everyone? What are you going to do to remind them of their intrinsic worth as a human being? You don't have to become everyone's friend, just show them a little gratitude, joy, or interest in their lives.

---

[1] "Dehumanize." Merriam-Webster, Merriam-Webster, 31 July 2018, www.merriam-webster.com/dictionary/dehumanize?utm_campaign=sd&utm_medium=serp&utm_source=jsonld.

Day 1 __/__/20__

Flex your empathy muscle. Sincerely ask someone about their day and actively listen when they answer. If you normally do this for friends, listen to someone you haven't listened to recently.

Day 2 __/__/20__

Look into who your local and state representatives are and how you can contact them. Follow your governor, House Representatives, and Senate representatives, and more on social media. You will be calling, emailing, and writing them later on this year, so you'll want to have the necessary information nearby.

Day 3 __/__/20__

Be aware of how language dehumanizes or rehumanizes our fellow human beings. Today, pay extra close attention to the terms and phrases those in media and in your everyday life use for other human beings. It's about how much dignity is afforded each human being, regardless of whether they are there to hear a comment.

Day 4 __/__/20__

Join the Rehumanize International Street Team Facebook group. There you will be provided with opportunities to help spread the Consistent Life Ethic & earn free swag while you do it! Points you earn each week can be exchanged for Rehumanize merchandise such as stickers, buttons, shirts, conference tickets & more!

Day 5 __/__/20__

With a group of friends or family, start to read a fiction or nonfiction book. In the back of this book we've provided a list of movies and books about the CLE in general and specific topics within it. Set a date to discuss among yourselves.

You will rehumanize everyone *consistently.*

"Those who defend the right to life of the weakest among us, must be equally visible in support of the quality of life of the powerless among us: the old and the young, the hungry and the homeless, the undocumented immigrant and the unemployed worker."
-Joseph Cardinal Bernardin, who popularized the Consistent Life Ethic[2]

The mainstream CLE concerns itself with 4 central forms of homicide: abortion, euthanasia, the death penalty, and unjust war.

These acts all:
1. Are threats to human's lives
2. Are acts of aggressive violence,
3. Have non-violent alternatives.

When reflecting on your own belief system, where are there gaps in consistency? Who are you leaving out?

_____

_____

_____

_____

---

[2] Bernardin, Cardinal. "EXCERPTS FROM CARDINAL BERNARDIN'S APPEAL FOR A 'CONSISTENT EHTIC OF LIFE'." The New York Times, The New York Times, 7 Dec. 1983, www.nytimes.com/1983/12/07/nyregion/excerpts-from-cardinal-bernardin-s-appeal-for-a-consistent-ehtic-of-life.html.

Day 6 __/__/20__

Find a favorite CLE-centered quote or Rehumanize International graphic to make your own. Rephrase it or just rewrite it in your own unique handwriting. Make it into a graphic for social media or a sign for the next march or protest you attend.

Day 7 __/__/20__

Start a conversation with someone you know who is against some but not all forms of legal homicide. While respecting their opinions and the life experiences that may have led to those opinions, question them on the inconsistency of their stances. Encourage them to really rethink their position.

Day 8 __/__/20__

Rehumanize yourself! Think about how you are best rejuvenated and relaxed. Do something today to take care of you and make yourself feel at peace.

Day 9 __/__/20__

If you have the money to do so, order stickers from Rehumanize to put on your computer, binders, water bottle, and then on light posts and such around town.

Day 10 __/__/20__

Choose some of your favorite CLE maxims. Look through this book or at online resources. Then get some chalk, choose a public place, and gather some pro-life, pro-peace friends. Share those nonviolent messages of life and justice with the world. Your consistency is radical in this polarized world, so don't be surprised if some opponents wash your messages away. For tips and more information check out *www.nationalprolifechalkday.com* .

Who you will rehumanize: human beings who are or have been incarcerated

"Consistent with previous years, the 2016 FBI Uniform Crime Report showed that the South had the highest murder rate. The South accounts for over 80% of executions. The Northeast, which has less than 1% of all executions, had lowest murder rate."

-Death Penalty Information Center[3]

Some would argue that capital punishment works to deter others from committing heinous crimes but there is no evidence to support that claim.

Think about capital punishment and start a dialogue.
Some talking points include: Why would we want the state to have the legal power to kill? In a civilized society such as ours aren't there better alternatives, such as restorative justice? There's no evidence that the death penalty deters crime. A criminal's actions, though wrong, do not undo his humanity or negate the inherent dignity due to him as a human being.

Your research:

_____

_____

_____

_____

---

[3] "Facts About the Death Penalty." Death Penalty Information Center, Death Penalty Information Center, 28 June 2018, deathpenaltyinfo.org//documents/FactSheet.pdf.

Day 11 __/__/20__

Do your own research about the legal history, demographics, and consequences of capital punishment in the U.S.

Day 12 __/__/20__

Look into the prison system in your state and the prisons near you. Are those on the inside treated with the respect due to human beings? Or are the conditions dehumanizing? Find out if there is an action committee or human rights group in your area that you could get involved in. What policies have been enacted by or voted for by the representatives you have or could vote for?

Day 13 __/__/20__

Get creative. Use what you've been learning about capital punishment and how you feel about it to make something artistic. There's no competition or grading, so just express yourself however you feel like it.

Day 14 __/__/20__

Read a short story or a true personal account. Invite someone else to read it as well so that you two can discuss the piece.

Day 15 __/__/20__

Check out organizations that connect prisoners and civilians to become a pen pal with someone suffering the difficult effects of isolation and dehumanization behind bars. One resource for this is *PrisonerCorrespondenceProject.com*. Think seriously about making this commitment before doing so.

Who you will rehumanize: preborn human beings and their parents

"Human development begins at fertilization, approximately 14 days after the onset of the last menstrual period... when a sperm fuses with an oocyte to form a single cell, the zygote. This highly specialized, totipotent cell marks the beginning of each of us as a unique individual."

- Keith L. Moore[4]

Sidewalk counseling is the practice of peacefully standing outside facilities that commit abortions, to offer life-affirming choices to patients before they enter.

Many, many people will have abortion experiences at some point in their lifetime, whether they were the one pregnant, or it was their partner, or maybe their sibling or grandchild or cousin was aborted. Organizations such as Rachel's Vineyard are imperative, that focus on healing people from all walks after they have lost someone to abortion.

---

[4] Moore, Keith L., et al. The Developing Human: Clinically Oriented Embryology. 10th ed., Elsevier, 2016.

Day 16 __/__/20__

Participate in an online or in-person training to sidewalk counsel (*www.rehumanizeintl.org/sidewalk-sidekicks*). It is very important that you learn to do this properly and with compassion, before going out with 40 Days for Life or another group.

Day 17 __/__/20__

Do some journaling. Reflect on your thoughts by spilling them out. This is one of many ways you can practice self-care.

Day 18 __/__/20__

Learn how to talk to someone who is post-abortive. The Project Rachel website (*http://hopeafterabortion.com/?p=103*) offers advice on this matter. Considering the number of post-abortive people out there, it's important for you to be able to respond compassionately when you find out someone has had an abortion.

Day 19 __/__/20__

Get to know local Planned Parenthood (PP) alternatives. Learn about the Pregnancy Resource Centers (PRC) and Federally Qualified Health Centers (FQHC) near you. Have contact info ready if you're sidewalk counseling or just talking to a person in need of life-affirming, affordable health care. Check *GetYourCare.org*

Day 20 __/__/20__

Sidewalk counsel in front of a PP or other facility. If this is your first time it's best to go on a day they are not performing abortions, just keep that in mind when you're there. Additionally, please make sure you will be with someone who is trained and has done it before. It can be nerve-wracking, but just remember that even if you don't feel 100% prepared, your presence will mean something.

Who you will rehumanize: human beings in abusive situations

Domestic violence hotline: 1-800-799-7233

1 in 4 women and 1 in 7 men experience domestic violence.

According to the National Domestic Violence Hotline website, "Domestic violence (also called intimate partner violence (IPV), domestic abuse or relationship abuse) is a pattern of behaviors used by one partner to maintain power and control over another partner in an intimate relationship."[5]

---

[5] "Abuse Defined." The National Domestic Violence Hotline, www.thehotline.org/is-this-abuse/abuse-defined/

Day 21 __/__/20__
Donate and paint your fingernail purple. Join the #PutTheNailInIt campaign to end domestic violence. Donate on the website *putthenailinit.com* then help them raise awareness by painting only your ring finger purple.

Day 22 __/__/20__
Analyze the media you consume. Does it perpetuate a culture of violence or demean women or other marginalized groups in any way? If your TV shows, video games, and such are not exemplifying a respect for human rights, consider why you are watching them.

Day 23 __/__/20__
Save the hotline number in your phone. If you hear a domestic disturbance in your neighborhood, do not ignore it. Contact the hotline or a local crisis center that can help defuse a situation.

Day 24 __/__/20__
Research local shelters and homes for women and children escaping abusive situations. Contact local shelters and find out how you can help or if they need donations

Day 25 __/__/20__
Volunteer at a local women's shelter.

**To *sonder* is to rehumanize -
to transfer our own understanding of how difficult
and beautiful and awful and awesome
it is to be human - for every single human being.**

Who you will rehumanize: human beings impacted by unjust wars

"The tradition of military ethics known as the Just War Theory holds that uses of military force:

1) must discriminate between military personnel and civilians and
2) must not cause so much harm as to outweigh whatever good the use of military force is intended to achieve.

Nearly all conceivable uses of nuclear weapons fail to meet either of these Just war requirements."
-John Whitehead[6]

Write about what you learn this week on war & PTSD:

_____ .

_____

_____

_____

"Non-violence is the greatest force at the disposal of mankind. It is mightier than the mightiest weapon of destruction devised by the ingenuity of man."
--Mahatma Gandhi[7]

---

[6] Whitehead, John. Toward the Abolition of Strategic Nuclear Weapons: A Just War Analysis of Total War. Toward the Abolition of Strategic Nuclear Weapons: A Just War Analysis of Total War, Life Matters Journal.

[7] "Mahatma Gandhi Quotes." BrainyQuote, Xplore,

Day 26 __/__/20__

Talk to a veteran. Don't force them to recall painful memories but do ask them about how they felt before, during, and after the war. Take the time to really listen.

Day 27 __/__/20__

Educate yourself on Post Traumatic Stress Disorder (PTSD) and other mental illnesses that affect veterans. Think about what you can do in your daily life to mitigate triggers of PTSD.

Day 28 __/__/20__

Go for a walk. Fresh air, exercise, and an opportunity to clear your head are always good for the health.

Day 29 __/__/20__

Follow #yemencantwait on social media to keep up with the effort to end the U.S.'s involvement in Saudi Arabia's war on Yemen. For more info and advice on how to call your senator about it, visit: *www.indivisible.org/resource/end-unauthorized-war-in-yemen.* To learn more and to sign a petition go to *stopthewar.us*.

Day 30 __/__/20__

Start another book, fiction or nonfiction, to read and discuss. You could choose a book about war, nuclear weapons, drone strikes, or another important CLE topic.

Who you will rehumanize: human beings victimized by human trafficking

Human Trafficking Hotline: 1 (888) 373-7888

Indicators of human trafficking:
Living with employer
Poor living conditions
Multiple people in cramped space
Inability to speak to individual alone
Answers appear to be scripted and rehearsed
Employer is holding identity documents
Signs of physical abuse
Submissive or fearful
Unpaid or paid very little
Under 18 and in prostitution[8]

"The only thing necessary for the triumph of evil is for good men to do nothing."
-Edmund Burke[9]

Notes from your research:

_____

_____

_____

---

[8] Identify and Assist a Trafficking Victim." U.S. Department of State, U.S. Department of State, www.state.gov/j/tip/id/index.htm.

[9] Colman, Dan. "'The Only Thing Necessary for the Triumph of Evil Is for Good Men to Do Nothing.' — Edmund Burke." Open Culture, 13 Mar. 2016, www.openculture.com/2016/03/edmund-burkeon-in-action.html.

Day 31 _/_/20_

Understand the many forms modern-slavery takes by exploring The CNN Freedom Project. You can also take the State Department's awareness training on their website.

Day 32 _/_/20_

Learn the warning signs of human trafficking. Think about where your products are made. Does your chocolate and coffee, for example, say it's fair trade certified? Visit *www.FairTradeCertified.org* to learn how to shop fair trade.

Day 33 _/_/20_

"Meet with and/or write to your local, state, and federal government representatives to let them know you care about combating human trafficking, and ask what they are doing to address it." –State Dept.[10]

Day 34 _/_/20_

Look into abolitionist organizations such as Love146 to find out how you can help them or to donate. The State Department website has a database of organizations you can get involved in locally.

Day 35 _/_/20_

Find out if your school includes modern slavery in its curriculum. If not, request that they change that, starting a petition if need be. Does your church have an awareness or victim support program? If not, who could start and continue to run one?

---

[10] "15 Ways You Can Help Fight Human Trafficking." *U.S. Department of State*, U.S. Department of State, www.state.gov/j/tip/id/help/index.htm.

Who you will rehumanize: human beings living with mental illness

National Suicide Prevention Lifeline: 1-800-273-8255

In America, 1 in 5 adults live with a mental illness.

"Nearly 60% of adults with a mental illness didn't receive mental health services in the previous year."[11]

Do you believe in or play into the stigmas around mental illness? Do you ever think of someone's mental health diagnosis as fake or insignificant? When you find out someone has a mental disorder do you distance yourself or treat them differently? How can you be more compassionate and helpful towards human beings in that situation?

_____

_____

_____

_____

_____

_____

[11] "Mental Health Facts in America." National Alliance on Mental Illness, www.nami.org/Learn-More/Mental-Health-By-the-Numbers.

Day 36 _/_/20_
At *suicidepreventionlifeline.org* learn about the risk factors and warning signs of suicide attempts.

Day 37 _/_/20_
Assess how you view mental illness. Do you see it as valid as any other physical illness? Do you discriminate against those with mental illness? If so, work to correct these.

Day 38 _/_/20_
#Bethe1to save a life! Join the movement to prepare yourself if you ever have the chance to help someone in crisis. Also, add the suicide prevention hotline number to your contacts for quick access.

Day 39 _/_/20_
Take care of your own mental health. Whether you're an introvert or an extrovert, do something today to recharge yourself.

Day 40 _/_/20_
Join an Out of the Darkness Community or Campus Walk through the American Foundation for Suicide Prevention. The money you raise can help with prevention efforts, support programs, and more.

We may encounter many defeats but we must not be defeated.
--Maya Angelou[12]

---

[12] "A Quote by Maya Angelou." *Goodreads*, Goodreads, www.goodreads.com/quotes/93512-you-may-encounter-many-defeats-but-you-must-not-be.

Who you will rehumanize: preborn human beings and their parents

According to information from the American College of Obstetricians and Gynecologists(ACOG) within the first trimester of gestation all of the fetus' major organ systems are developing and they can begin to hear and swallow.[13]

According to the CDC "The majority of abortions in 2014 took place early in gestation: 91.5% of abortions were performed at ≤13 weeks' gestation; a smaller number of abortions (7.2%) were performed at 14–20 weeks' gestation"[14]

How do our laws fail to support mothers, parents, and families? What are the parental leave laws/standards in your state?

_____

_____

_____

**"Abortion is the ultimate exploitation of women."
-Alice Paul[15],
feminist foremother, suffragist, author of
the Equal Rights Amendment**

---

[13] "How Your Fetus Grows During Pregnancy." *American College of Obstetricians and Gynecologists*, ACOG, Apr. 2018, www.acog.org/Patients/FAQs/How-Your-Fetus-Grows-During-Pregnancy#one.
[14] "Reproductive Health." *Centers for Disease Control and Prevention*, Centers for Disease Control and Prevention, 16 Nov. 2017, www.cdc.gov/reproductivehealth/data_stats/abortion.htm.
[15] "'Abortion Is the Ultimate Exploitation of Women.'" *Human Coalition*, www.humancoalition.org/graphics/abortion-ultimate-exploitation-women/.

Day 41 _/_/20_

Watch a pro-life movie. *Bella* is a well-known one and we've provided a movie list in the back of this book, but you can look up a list of others. Invite family or friends to watch with you.

Day 42 _/_/20_

Learn about single parenting, pregnancy, and more. Ask someone in your life that has been a single parent what it's like. Ask your mom or another mother what it's like to be pregnant, especially if they have experienced an unplanned pregnancy. Try to understand the financial, social, physical, and emotional struggles of pregnancy.

Day 43 _/_/20_

Write a poem about the preborn or another marginalized group.

Day 44 _/_/20_

Find some pro-life feminist answers to pro-choice arguments. Check out the websites of Feminists for Life and Rehumanize International (*www.rehumanizeintl.org*) and consider doing a specifically pro-life feminist outreach event in your community.

Day 45 _/_/20_

Volunteer at your local Pregnancy Resource Center/Crisis Pregnancy Center. Tasks might be as simple as cleaning, organizing, or envelope stuffing. Ask about writing a letter to a birth mom or providing some other support, or even throwing a baby shower for teen moms.

Who you will rehumanize: elderly human beings

There are many logical, sensible arguments against euthanasia and Physician Assisted Suicide (PAS), but at the heart of the issue is the fact that some human's lives (those who are "more abled") are culturally valued more than others. This is an obvious sign of injustice.

Talking points and arguments against euthanasia & PAS:

_____

_____

_____

_____

**"I feel the duty to reaffirm strongly that
the intrinsic value and personal dignity
of every human being do not change,
no matter the concrete circumstances of [their] life.
A man, even if seriously ill or disabled
in the exercise of his highest functions,
is and always will be a man,
and he will never become a 'vegetable' or an 'animal'."
–Pope John Paul II**[16]

---

[16] Pope John Paul. "Congress on Life-Sustaining Treatments and Vegetative State." *Eternal Word Television Network*, L'Osservatore Romano English Edition, 31 Mar. 2004, www.ewtn.com/library/PAPALDOC/JP2LIFSS.HTM.

Day 46 _/_/20_

Check the Rehumanize International website, *propeaceprolife.org*, to find out the date of the next Rehumanize Conference. Add it to your calendar, so you can start planning to attend. It is an incredible weekend event dedicated to education, discourse, activism and volunteerism related to a broad range of issues of human rights and dignity!

Day 47 _/_/20_

Learn the arguments against euthanasia. Check out the Euthanasia Prevention Coalition.

Day 48 _/_/20_

Reconnect with an elderly person in your life. The aged often feel lonely, forgotten, and unimportant, and a quick phone call, letter, or outing together might go a long way toward their mental health and feelings of self-worth.

Day 49 _/_/20_

Collect stories for Encounter Youniverse.

At *www.encounteryouniverse.com/* you can share a personal story of your own or help others share theirs. You can also record some stories from the folks you meet at a nearby nursing home on Day 50.

Day 50 _/_/20_

Visit a nearby nursing home. You'll have to contact a conveniently located assisted living community about their rules and processes for volunteers. Also, ask them about bringing a group with you next time.

Who you will rehumanize: human beings with physical disabilities

"Of spinal cord injured high-level quadriplegics, 86% rated their quality of life as average or better. Only 17% of their medical staff thought they could have an average or better quality of life"[17]

Our worth is not based on our circumstances but in our shared humanity.

Your research on the laws regarding Physician Assisted Suicide:

_____

_____

_____

_____

_____

_____

_____

_____

[17] MacNair, Rachel M, and Stephen Zunes. *Consistently Opposing Killing: from Abortion to Assisted Suicide, the Death Penalty, and War.* Authors Choice Press, 2008.

Day 51 _/_/20_

Get to know someone with a disability. Whether just going out of your way in day to day life to get to know a new friend, or joining a disability rights organization, pursue solidarity with the individuals in this often-marginalized group by asking how you can amplify their voices by using your own privilege to aid in advocacy alongside them in search for justice.

Day 52 _/_/20_

If you're able to, do some cardio: walk, jog, do jumping jacks, do sit-ups, dance, kickbox, play a sport. You can't take care of others without first taking care of yourself.

Day 53 _/_/20_

Research the laws or proposed policies in your state regarding Physician Assisted Suicide (PAS). You may come across euphemisms such as "aid in dying" or "death with dignity"

Day 54 _/_/20_

Write your representatives about disability rights in your state.

Day 55 _/_/20_

I hope you have been doing well with your reading. I'm going to suggest you and a friend or a group start a new book! Maybe in your work this year you've heard some reading recommendations you could pick, or you can choose from the many options listed at the back of this book.

Who you will rehumanize: immigrant and refugee human beings

According to the UNHCR, in 2017, 68.5 million people were forcibly displaced from their homes worldwide.[18]

The president of the International Rescue Committee, David Miliband, gave a TedTalk in 2017 on his solutions to the global refugee crisis. He gave four solutions:

- "Refugees need to be able to work.

- Education for refugee kids should be a lifeline, not a luxury.

- Refugees need money.

- The most vulnerable refugees need the chance to start a new life in the West."[19]

<u>Write about what you're finding out:</u>

_____

_____

_____

_____

---

[18] United Nations. "Figures at a Glance." *UNHCR*, UNHCR, 19 June 2018, www.unhcr.org/en-us/figures-at-a-glance.html.

[19] "TED2017: David Miliband's 4 Solutions to Ending the Global Refugee Crisis." *International Rescue Committee (IRC)*, International Rescue Committee (IRC), 20 June 2017

Day 56 __/__/20__
At *Rescue.org* and through other sources, learn about the myths many Americans may believe about refugees. Find out about the vetting process to be accepted in the U.S. as a refugee and about the lives families leave behind to find safety and security in a new country.

Day 57 __/__/20__
Look into aid organizations such as the UNHCR, the UN Refugee Agency; the U.S. Committee for Refugees and Immigrants; and the International Rescue Committee. Choose a nonprofit to donate to (preferably one that doesn't support other forms of violence!).

Day 58 __/__/20__
Learn about immigration policy and reform. Educate yourself on the laws that impact people in your community and how those laws are enacted.

Day 59 __/__/20__
Sign a petition in support of safety and human rights for refugees and/or immigrants. Share the petition or a shareable graphic on social media using appropriate hashtags.

Day 60 __/__/20__
Volunteer to work with immigrants and refugees. At your community center or a local refugee resettlement office or charity, try assistant teaching ESL classes or a citizenship course.

Who you will rehumanize: human beings experiencing homelessness

When you have a chance to interact with someone who is asking for money or utilizing some aid for the homeless population, be sure to treat them like you would want to be treated. When you can give them something, take the time to stop what you're doing, introduce yourself and ask their name, and inquire about their day, their dog (if they have one), or perhaps their favorite snack. And if you can't, remember that they are still human beings with inherent dignity. Consider stopping to talk, and always give a smile and apologize sincerely. Courtesy and kindness can go a long way on the sidewalks and some of the people you meet may rarely ever hear their name said out loud.

Sonder -
The realization that each random passerby is living a life as vivid and complex as your own.[20]

---

[20]John Koenig. "Sonder Definition" Dictionary of Obscure Sorrows, 2012, http://www.dictionaryofobscuresorrows.com/post/23536922667/sonder

Day 61 __/__/20__
Have water bottles in your car to hand out to day laborers or those experiencing homelessness.

Day 62 __/__/20__
Find out about local charities and organizations that assist the homeless population in your area or nearby.

Day 63 __/__/20__
Write about a Consistent Life Ethic topic and submit it to Rehumanize International for our blog. Email Herb, our Director of Communications, at herb@rehumanizeintl.org.

Day 64 __/__/20__
Brighten your own day. Call an old friend. Or a new one.

Day 65 __/__/20__
Volunteer at a soup kitchen or another resource for the homeless, but make sure to strike up at least one real conversation with someone you're serving.

"We shall never know the good that a simple smile can do."
−Mother Teresa[21]

---

[21] "Mother Teresa Quotes." *BrainyQuote*, BrainyQuote, www.brainyquote.com/quotes/mother_teresa_125711.

Who you will rehumanize: preborn human beings and their parents

How we talk about adoption as a legitimate, life-affirming, and responsible choice makes a huge difference in the lives of birth parents, especially if they are still unsure what they will do about their unexpected baby.

American Adoptions offers these pieces of advice for the best way to refer to different aspects of adoption:

Negative: Real parent
Positive: Birth parent, birth mother, birth father

Negative: Give up/give away child for adoption
Positive: Place child for adoption, make an adoption plan

Negative: To keep
Positive: To parent

Negative: Unwanted child
Positive: Child placed for adoption

Negative: Is adopted
Positive: Was adopted

Negative: Adoptive parent
Positive: Parent[22]

---

[22] "A New Year's Resolution: Using Positive Adoption Language." *American Adoptions*, 11 Jan. 2012. Web.

Day 66 __/__/20__

Pay attention to your attitude toward parents experiencing an unplanned pregnancy. Don't write off women in those situations as lost causes. When you hear about or are talking to someone facing an unplanned pregnancy, take the opportunity to reach out, offer resources, support, and congratulations.

Day 67 __/__/20__

Become an advocate for birth mothers and a better adoption process for all people involved. According to their website, BraveLove is a "pro-adoption movement dedicated to changing the perception of adoption by acknowledging birth moms for their brave decision."[23] With this organization or another, get involved.

Day 68 __/__/20__

Bring up the issue of abortion with a person or group you wouldn't normally. It's easy to be pro-life around pro-lifers but how can you show the truth to people who are on the fence? Be tactful and sensitive, of course.

Day 69 __/__/20__

Look up the date and locations of an upcoming March for Life in a city near you or the national one in Washington, DC. Add it to a calendar you will check or make a reminder on your phone (far enough ahead of time to prepare).

Day 70 __/__/20__

Educate yourself on proposed laws or open court cases in your state regarding abortion and adoption.

---

[23] "BraveLove." *BraveLove*, www.bravelove.org/.

Who you will rehumanize: human beings at the embryonic stage of development

"Embryonic stem cells are derived from embryos at a developmental stage before the time that implantation would normally occur in the uterus."[24] We, as humans, do not gain human dignity when we are born; when we, as fetuses, start looking "cute" like babies; or at any particular point in our development. Equality among all human beings must begin as soon as a human being comes into existence, whether naturally or in a lab.

Notes from your research this week:

_____

_____

_____

_____

"A human life is a human life;
and if equality means anything, it means that society
may not value some human lives over others."
-Mary Meehan[25]

---

[24] Thomson, James A, and Junying Yu. "Embryonic Stem Cells." *National Institutes of Health*, U.S. Department of Health and Human Services, stemcells.nih.gov/info/Regenerative_Medicine/2006Chapter1.htm.

[25] MacNair, Rachel, and Stephen Zunes. *Consistently Opposing Killing: from Abortion to Assisted Suicide, the Death Penalty, and War.* Authors Choice Press, 2011.

Day 71 __/__/20__

Research the latest on Stem Cell Research (SCR). Teach yourself about adult and embryonic SCR for future discussions and to better understand the debate. Check out *StemCellResearch.org*.

Day 72 __/__/20__

Find and sign a petition against further funding and experimentation with Embryonic Stem Cells. If you can't find one, start one. You can use *Change.org*.

Day 73 __/__/20__

Rehumanize yourself. You could read a heartwarming story that will lift your spirits.

Day 74 __/__/20__

Learn about embryo adoption. According to the Embryo Adoption Awareness Center, "embryo donation and adoption is a proven successful process allowing families with remaining embryos to donate them to another family desiring to experience pregnancy and childbirth."[26] Consider the ethical ramifications of "donating" children and how we can rehumanize these children that nonetheless have inherent human dignity.

Day 75 __/__/20__

After finding out about laws and funding of ESCR contact your government officials. Talk about what should change or what they are doing about it or even just asking them to think about it if they haven't.

---

[26] "Home Page." *Embryo Adoption Awareness Center*, U.S. Department of Health and Human Services, www.embryoadoption.org/.

Who you will rehumanize: human beings with disabilities or terminal illnesses

When the state declares that if someone has a terminal prognosis they should have the right to commit suicide, it has been shown that this is indeed is not far from saying that anyone who has such a prognosis *should* commit suicide. Some individuals with terminal diagnoses have had palliative and life-lengthening care denied by state-sponsored insurance plans, but instead have been offered prescriptions for assisted suicide medication.[27]

In the abstract of the article, "Non-Faith-Based Arguments Against Physician-Assisted Suicide and Euthanasia" the authors state, "here are four non-religious, reasonable arguments against physician-assisted suicide and euthanasia: (1) 'it offends me,' suicide devalues human life; (2) slippery slope, the limits on euthanasia gradually erode; (3) 'pain can be alleviated,' palliative care and modern therapeutics more and more adequately manage pain; (4) physician integrity and patient trust, participating in suicide violates the integrity of the physician and undermines the trust patients place in physicians to heal and not to harm."[28]

---

[27] Richardson, Bradford. "Assisted-suicide law prompts insurance company to deny coverage to terminally ill California woman." Washington Times, October 20, 2016.
www.washingtontimes.com/news/2016/oct/20/assisted-suicide-law-prompts-insurance-company-den/

[28] Sulmasy, Daniel P., et al. "Non-Faith-Based Arguments against Physician-Assisted Suicide and Euthanasia." *National Center for Biotechnology Information,* The Linacre Quarterly, Aug. 2016, www.ncbi.nlm.nih.gov/pmc/articles/PMC5102187/.

Day 76 _/_/20_

Make a sign or digital graphic. You might find an event to bring your sign to, or you might be able to spark a conversation by posting your graphic online. Choose words that are life-affirming and are clearly against euthanasia and Physician Assisted Suicide (PAS).

Day 77 _/_/20_

Take a picture with it your sign and post on social media. Use this as an opportunity to find out other people's thoughts on the issue of PAS and euthanasia.

Day 78 _/_/20_

Read a personal story from someone with a terminal prognosis or disability.

Day 79 _/_/20_

Find out when the Special Olympics will be this year and keep up with them. Share about it on social media.

Day 80 _/_/20_

Volunteer with a camp or day program for adults or children with disabilities. Learn more about them and their life experiences.

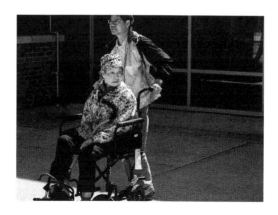

Who you will rehumanize: human beings experiencing homelessness

According to the National Alliance to End Homelessness, "There are an estimated 553,742 people in the United States experiencing homelessness on a given night, according to the most recent national point-in-time estimate (January 2017)."[29]

"Being homeless is like living in a post-apocalyptic world. You're on the outskirts of society." -Frank Dillane[30]

What have you learned about what your local gov't & community is doing to help those experiencing homelessness?

_____

_____

_____

_____

_____

_____

[29] "The State of Homelessness in America." *National Alliance to End Homelessness*, endhomelessness.org/homelessness-in-america/homelessness-statistics/state-of-homelessness-report/.

[30] Miller, Adam. "EXCLUSIVE: Fear The Walking Dead's Frank Dillane Avoided Watching Dad in Game of Thrones." *Express.co.uk*, Express.co.uk, 24 Mar. 2016

Day 81 __/__/20__
Time to start another book. When you discuss this book, with the same group as before or a new one, challenge yourselves to delve deeper into the content, characters, or morals of the story.

Day 82 __/__/20__
Rehumanize yourself. Relax by watching a favorite movie from your childhood again.

Day 83 __/__/20__
Stop what you're doing to buy a hot/cold drink for someone asking for help on the street. Find out their name and how they are doing.

Day 84 __/__/20__
Find out: how is your local government involved in helping people who are facing poverty?

Day 85 __/__/20__
Volunteer with Habitat for Humanity for the day. Invite some friends to join you.

Human beings have dignity and worth not because of what they can do, but because of what they are and more importantly, because of who they are.

Who you will rehumanize: preborn human beings and their parents

According to a summary of National Geographic's 2005 film *In the Womb*, "the development of all of these complex functions prior to birth has also led some experts to posit that, developmentally, birth is not as significant as was previously assumed."

-The Embryo Project Encyclopedia[31]

"Abortion should be listed as a weapon of mass destruction against the voiceless."
— E.A. Bucchianeri[32]

---

[31] Maayan, Inbar. "In the Womb (2005), by Toby Mcdonald and National Geographic Channel." *The Embryo Project Encyclopedia*, Arizona State University, 7 Apr. 2015.

[32] "Abortion Should Be Listed As A Weapon Of MASS DESTRUCTION Against The VOICELESS." *Human Coalition*, www.humancoalition.org/graphics/abortion-should-be-listed-as-a-weapon-of-mass-destruction-agai nst-the-voiceless/.

Day 86 __/__/20__

Learn the arguments against "unwantedness". It is a common pro-abortion slogan that with abortion no child will be an unwanted child. The fact is, how wanted or loved someone is doesn't change their intrinsic worth as a human being.

Day 87 __/__/20__

Invite someone to the March for Life you plan to go to, whether local or national. It can be a powerful experience for someone, especially if they are pro-life but don't really act on it.

Day 88 __/__/20__

Memorize the major fetal development milestones. Speaking in terms of time since LMP (last menstrual period), known as gestational age, is the norm for referring to fetal development.

Day 89 __/__/20__

Figure out the date of national pro-life T-shirt day. Buy or make a shirt for the occasion. Rehumanize International, Students for Life of America, and *Abort73.com* all sell great pro-life apparel.

Day 90 __/__/20__

Offer to babysit for free. Find out through the Pregnancy Resource Center you worked with previously if there's anyone in need of a babysitter. Otherwise, extend the helpful offer to a neighbor, classmate, friend, or acquaintance.

Who you will rehumanize: human beings being tortured and unjustly detained

According to an infographic from the ACLU, over 200 FBI agents have reported abuse of Guantanamo detainees.

It also states that of the 40 prisoners detained at GITMO 5 have been cleared for release and 26 have not been cleared for release or charged with any crime![33]

Witness Against Torture provides some ideas for talking points on their "Join Us" page:

- "Each Guantánamo detainee must either be charged and fairly tried in federal court, or be released to countries that will respect their human rights.
- Expedite the release of those that are cleared.
- Release the men who have been tortured.
- Provide reasonable resettlement options,
- Publicly acknowledge and apologize .
- Close the base." [34]

**"True peace is not merely the absence of tension, but the presence of justice."
-Martin Luther King Jr.[35]**

---

[33] "Guantánamo by the Numbers." *American Civil Liberties Union*, American Civil Liberties Union, www.aclu.org/issues/national-security/detention/guantanamo-numbers?redirect=infographic/guant anamo-numbers.

[34] "Join Us." *Witness Against Torture*, New York Catholic Worker, www.witnessagainsttorture.com/join-us/.

[35] "'When Peace Becomes Obnoxious.'" *The Martin Luther King, Jr., Research and Education Institute*, Stanford University, 18 Mar. 1956,

Day 91 __/__/20__

Look into Guantanamo Bay then call/write a government official. Witness Against Torture states that you can contact your Senate or House representatives, the U.S. Embassy in Cuba, or Southern Command which oversees the prison. With the inhumane treatment going on there it needs to be shut down. If your elected official is against closing Guantanamo, then write them about it. If your elected official supports closing Guantanamo but hasn't done anything about it, write them, too!

Day 92 __/__/20__

On Fridays, give up something you enjoy, (perhaps like social media, sweet treats, or eating out) in solidarity with the participants on hunger strike at Guantanamo. Learn more about efforts to end torture at *www.witnessagainsttorture.com/join-us/*.

Day 93 __/__/20__

Check yourself on the negative/positive balance of your attitude and self-talk. It is hard to improve on how others are seen by society if you do not see your own human dignity.

Day 94 __/__/20__

Make a sign or graphic and share it on social media. Spread some knowledge!

Day 95 __/__/20__

Talk to someone or read a personal account of someone who was a Prisoner Of War, especially if they were a prisoner of the U.S. Ask questions, if they're willing. Witness Against Torture has a resource list on their website with reading suggestions.

---

kinginstitute.stanford.edu/king-papers/documents/when-peace-becomes-obnoxious.

Who you will rehumanize: human beings victimized by racism

Systematic racism is prevalent in most aspects of everyday life. African Americans and other racial minorities face racism when it comes to their education, healthcare, right to privacy, housing and employment availability, opportunities for economic advancement, and rights in the face of the criminal justice system.

According to the U.S. Department of Education Office for Civil Rights, "black students are suspended and expelled at a rate three times greater than white students. On average, 5% of white students are suspended, compared to 16% of black students."[36]

"Darkness cannot drive out darkness; only light can do that. Hate cannot drive out hate; only love can do that."
-Martin Luther King Jr[37]

What subtle racism did you observe this week in yourself or others?

_____

_____

_____

[36] United States, Congress, Office for Civil Rights. "CIVIL RIGHTS DATA COLLECTION Data Snapshot: School Discipline." *CIVIL RIGHTS DATA COLLECTION Data Snapshot: School Discipline*, 2014.

[37] Evers, Myrlie. "Martin Luther King, Jr. Day Reflections." Evers Institute, 18 Jan. 2016, www.eversinstitute.org/featured-post/martin-luther-king-jr-day/.

Day 96 __/__/20__
Re-evaluate yourself and your thinking. Think seriously and don't write off racism as not affecting you. Pay attention to underlying biases and prejudices you may hold.

Day 97 __/__/20__
Strive to understand how and why racism is still a problem in America. Research the causes and effects. Talk to someone of another race or ethnicity than you and/or a person of color.

Day 98 __/__/20__
Research influential court cases within the topic of America's long battle with and fight for equal civil rights. What can we learn from the past? What might the future bring?

Day 99 __/__/20__
Find a song about race or racism (or another CLE issue). Share it with someone and discuss. All these discussions do not need to be stuffy, capital "D" Discussions; casual but thoughtful conversations are impactful too.

Day 100 __/__/20__
Day One Hundred! It's time to challenge the pessimist in you. Think of or find 100 ways the world has improved for people in the last century. You can also add to the list ways in which humans are respectful of each other and generally good for the world.

Who you will rehumanize: immigrant and refugee human beings

According to the UNHCR, "By the end of 2017, 68.5 million individuals were forcibly displaced worldwide as a result of persecution, conflict, violence or human rights violations."

Syria has the largest number of forcibly displaced persons, more than half their population, at a total of 12 million at the end of 2016[38]

Write about what you've found out this week & how it made you feel:

_____

_____

_____

_____

_____

_____

_____

_____

---

[38] "Refugee Statistics ." *USA for UNHCR*, www.unrefugees.org/refugee-facts/statistics/.

Day 101 _/_/20_

Learn about proposed national immigration reform/law. What are different government officials saying about it? What needs to be done so that it does or does not go into effect.

Day 102 _/_/20_

Write to your representatives about the proposed law, or one already imposed. Ask someone who agrees with you on the issue about how to get through to government officials.

Day 103 _/_/20_

Take today to clear your mind. Declutter a space that you use often. You may be surprised how refreshing it can be.

Day 104 _/_/20_

Reflect on xenophobia, the lives of refugees and immigrants, stories you may have heard, etc. Paint something based on all of that, or create some other form of art.

Day 105 _/_/20_

After looking into different organizations choose one to fundraise for. This can take the form of just asking them how you can help them raise money or start a campaign of your own.

Who you will rehumanize: preborn human beings and their parents

The pro-life movement often gets accused of being "pro-birth" and of not caring for the baby after they are born or even of not caring about the mother once she has chosen life for her child. In the past, and with a certain sect of pro-lifers this may be true. However, we are youthful and more able than anyone to change the face of this movement for the better. Women, children, and families deserve a culture that will support them and uphold their dignity holistically.

Pregnancy Resource Centers, if run properly, are pro-women support resources. They exist, not only to help pregnant people choose life, but to offer material goods such as baby clothes and diapers and counseling services. Pro-lifers should be rallying for services and laws that will make the prospect of having a child you didn't plan on less overwhelming and the costs of choosing adoption less cumbersome.

"In 2011, 42% of unintended pregnancies (excluding miscarriages) ended in abortion, and 58% ended in birth. This was a small shift from 2008, when 40% ended in abortion and 60% ended in birth." –Guttmacher Institute[39]

<u>Reflect on how you would respond if a friend confided to you that they were facing an unplanned pregnancy:</u>

_____

_____

---

[39] "Unintended Pregnancy in the United States." *Guttmacher Institute*, 20 Sept. 2017, www.guttmacher.org/fact-sheet/unintended-pregnancy-united-states.

Day 106 __/__/20__

Go to *SaveTheOne.org*. Learn the pro-life case against the "rape exception" argument, which says that if the mother of a preborn baby conceived through rape that it should be legal to abort that child.

Day 107 __/__/20__

Start to read a fiction or nonfiction book about abortion, unplanned pregnancy, adoption, etc. Make sure to set a date to discuss with others what you read.

Day 108 __/__/20__

Plan to make Sidewalk Counseling "Blessing Bags" to have ready for when you will sidewalk counsel outside an abortion facility next week. Check out *www.rehumanizeintl.org/sidewalk-sidekicks* for downloadable pamphlets and drop cards you can buy.

Day 109 __/__/20__

Order Sidewalk Sidekicks resources. Review anything you learned the day you sidewalk counseled on a non-abortion day, because this time your challenge is to go out on an abortion day.

Day 110 __/__/20__

Lead a Sidewalk Sidekicks training for a group, at the end of next week you and your group can put what you learned to action. Ask and answer questions. Practice dialoguing with each other what you would say in different situations.

Who you will rehumanize: preborn human beings and their parents

"In 2011, nearly half (45% or 2.8 million) of the 6.1 million pregnancies in the United States each year were unintended."

"In 2014, three-fourths of abortion patients were low income—49% living at less than the federal poverty level, and 26% living at 100–199% of the poverty level."-Guttmacher Institute[40]

In other words, the pro-life movement has quite a lot of people that could use our help. There are hundreds of organizations nationwide that exist to provide that support, but they need all of our help. If we expect all those women to give birth we should be lobbying for better standards of family leave, affordable housing and child-care services, and child support. We must make sure women are empowered by educating them on their rights, their resources, and the rights of their child.

Feminism has always celebrated all that women are capable of. That means validating and encouraging the brave choice to select an adoptive family for her child or the brave choice to parent, especially if she is going to be a single parent.

---

[40]Jerman, Jenna, et al. "Characteristics of U.S. Abortion Patients in 2014 and Changes Since 2008." *Guttmacher Institute*, 10 June 2016, www.guttmacher.org/report/characteristics-us-abortion-patients-2014.

Day 111 _/_/20_

Write a letter to a strong mom. Through Embrace Grace's "Love Box" initiative you can write a thoughtful note to a mother who chose life and needs your support.

Day 112 _/_/20_

Play a game. Do something fun for yourself. Invite friends or hang out with cousins (if you have any).

Day 113 _/_/20_

It's time to put together those sidewalk counseling "blessing bags". Make sure that they include a list of nearby resources such as PRCs and FQHC and their contact info.

Day 114 _/_/20_

Learn the arguments against prenatal diagnosis being a justifiable reason to abort. It must be extremely difficult for pregnant parents to find out that their baby's life may be brief, but there are perinatal hospice services for parents so that they can spend as much time with their newborn as possible and help the child be as pain-free as possible.

Day 115 _/_/20_

Today you will sidewalk counsel on an abortion day. You should never do this alone. Try to connect with a school club, church group, state right to life organization, or 40 Days for Life chapter. You are well prepared and practice will be the main way you can grow in skill at this task.

Who you will rehumanize: human beings living with mental illness

"Depression affects 20-25% of Americans ages 18+ in a given year. (CDC)

The highest suicide rates in the US are among Whites, American Indians and Alaska Natives."[41]

<u>What did you learn this week about mental health care?</u>

_____

_____

_____

_____

_____

_____

_____

_____

---

[41] "Suicide Statistics and Facts ." *SAVE*, save.org/about-suicide/suicide-facts/.

Day 116 __/__/20__
Look into organizations to see where you can volunteer and how you can help. Some organizations to look at are: National Alliance on Mental Illness, Suicide Prevention Lifeline, American Foundation for Suicide Prevention, Suicide Awareness Voices of Education.

Day 117 __/__/20__
Write a song. Be creative and express yourself and the issues of mental health stigma or something else related.

Day 118 __/__/20__
Find a song, share, discuss. Try to find something with a positive message, maybe about getting help if you need it.

Day 119 __/__/20__
Look into how the government, state or federal, funds mental health care. Is it enough? Can it be improved? How?

Day 120 __/__/20__
Call or write a government official about improvements. Maybe the Department of Health and Human Services could be doing more. You don't have to know everything about an issue, just demonstrate that this issue matters to your representative's constituents.

Who you will rehumanize: human beings impacted by unjust wars

"Given that the bombs that devastated Hiroshima and Nagasaki had yields in the range of 15-20 kilotons, using almost any warhead in current nuclear arsenals against a populated areas would cause massive indiscriminate death and destruction."

- John Whitehead[42]

"On July 7, 2017 the United Nations voted overwhelmingly to ban nuclear weapons altogether. The U.S. government did not even participate in the negotiations and did not participate in the vote. PNC Bank has loaned over $600,000,000 dollars to six corporations who manufacture nuclear weapons."

- *stopbankingthebomb.org*[43]

"Stand up for what is right even if you're standing alone." - Suzy Kassem[44]

---

[42] Whitehead, John. *Toward the Abolition of Strategic Nuclear Weapons: A Just War Analysis of Total War. Toward the Abolition of Strategic Nuclear Weapons: A Just War Analysis of Total War*, Life Matters Journal.

[43] "Home Page." *Stop Banking the Bomb*, stopbankingthebomb.org/.

[44] "A Quote from Rise Up and Salute the Sun." *Goodreads*, Goodreads, www.goodreads.com/quotes/7612928-stand-up-for-what-is-right-even-if-you-re-standing.

Day 121 _/_/20_

Read our white paper "Toward the Abolition of Strategic Nuclear Weapons" on the Rehumanize International website: *www.rehumanizeintl.org/nukes.*

Day 122 _/_/20_

Color or do some other type of art to rehumanize yourself. Maybe reflect on the impact of nuclear weapons or of drone warfare and how they create refugees.

Day 123 _/_/20_

Through online platforms or local protests, call out PNC bank or other financial institutions who back loans to nuclear weapons manufacturers. Insist that they stop banking the bomb!

Day 124 _/_/20_

Watch a movie about war and discuss. If you can, discuss it with someone who has experienced war.

Day 125 _/_/20_

Volunteer with veterans. Contact your local VA or other veterans center and offer your services for an upcoming event or other volunteer opportunity.

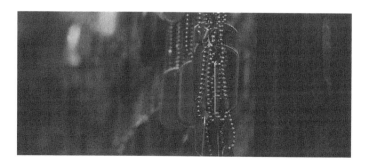

Who you will rehumanize: human beings with disabilities or terminal illness

According to the CNN Library, "Oregon - Has had a physician-assisted suicide law on the books since 1997. Since its enactment, there has been a steady increase in both prescription recipients and the number of deaths."[45] Oregon's Death with Dignity Act applies to terminally ill patients, not those suffering because of their advanced age or disability, however the statistics bear it out that PAS is most often used for very ableist reasons.

<u>What did you learn about the connection between ableism, prenatal diagnosis, euthanasia, and abortion?</u>

_____

_____

_____

_____

_____

_____

_____

_____

[45] "Physician-Assisted Suicide Fast Facts." *CNN*, Cable News Network, 4 June 2018, www.cnn.com/2014/11/26/us/physician-assisted-suicide-fast-facts/index.html.

Day 126 _/_/20_
Look into how accessible your city or neighborhood is for people with disabilities. Think about those who are deaf, those who are blind, and those who require mobility aids.

Day 127 _/_/20_
Learn arguments against the use of prenatal diagnoses of deformation or disability as justification for abortion. Seek info from organizations like the International Down Syndrome Coalition for Life to hear directly from disability rights activists who speak out about the intersection of ableism and abortion.

Day 128 _/_/20_
Wear a Rehumanize International shirt. If someone compliments you on it or asks about it, take the opportunity to introduce them to the Consistent Life Ethic.

Day 129 _/_/20_
Make a sketch or drawing. Use whatever artistic skills you may have to showcase the inherent dignity of every person no matter what their circumstances.

Day 130 _/_/20_
Watch a movie related to disability rights and discuss its message.

Who you will rehumanize: elderly human beings and those with terminal illnesses

Currently in 2018, in the District of Columbia and six U.S. states: Colorado, Washington, Oregon, Montana, Hawaii, and Vermont, a doctor cannot legally be prosecuted for writing a prescription for a medication with the intent to hasten death. Throughout these states the patient requesting "aid-in-dying" medication must be terminally ill and have a six months or less to live prognosis.[46]

Some terms to know the difference between:

"Voluntary active euthanasia – hastening one's own death by use of drugs or other means, with a doctor's direct assistance.

Passive euthanasia – hastening death by withdrawing life-sustaining treatment and letting nature take its course.

Involuntary euthanasia – causing or hastening the death of someone who has not asked for assistance with dying, such as a patient who has lost consciousness and is unlikely to regain it or who lacks decision-making capacity for other reasons."[47]

---

[46] "Physician-Assisted Suicide Fast Facts." *CNN*, Cable News Network, 4 June 2018, www.cnn.com/2014/11/26/us/physician-assisted-suicide-fast-facts/index.html.

[47] Quill, Timothy E., and Bernard Sussman. "Physician Assisted Death." *The Hastings Center*, www.thehastingscenter.org/briefingbook/physician-assisted-death/.

Day 131 __/__/20__
You know the drill: read a book and once you've finished, discuss it with others.

Day 132 __/__/20__
Compliment or commend yourself three separate times today. Boost your self-confidence and decimate negative self-talk.

Day 133 __/__/20__
Wear a pro-life t-shirt just for the fun of it. Take a picture of yourself wearing it. This is an easy way to spread the pro-life message.

Day 134 __/__/20__
Post on a social media account a picture of you in your shirt. Add in the caption some related information.

Day 135 __/__/20__
Make blankets for nursing home residents. If you aren't skilled at knitting or something similar, just look up the simple instructions for making fleece tie blankets. Have a plan for how the blankets can be labeled with the residents' names.

Who you will rehumanize: human beings who are or have been incarcerated

"Restorative justice is a theory of justice that emphasizes repairing the harm caused by criminal behaviour. It is best accomplished through cooperative processes that include all stakeholders. This can lead to transformation of people, relationships and communities."
—Centre for Justice and Reconciliation[48]

What have you learned this week?

_____

_____

_____

_____

_____

_____

"Since 1973, more than 162 people have been released from death row with evidence of their innocence."
-Staff Report, House Judiciary Subcommittee on Civil & Constitutional Rights, 1993, with updates by DPIC[49]

---

[48] Centre for Justice & Reconciliation. "Tutorial: Introduction to Restorative Justice." *Restorative Justice*, Prison Fellowship International

[49] "Facts about the Death Penalty." Death Penalty Information Center, 18 July 2018.

Day 136 __/__/20__

Learn about Perpetration Induced Traumatic Stress (PITS). Think about how this might relate both to the convicted offender, but also to prison guards, physicians who would have to administer the lethal injection, and more.

Day 137 __/__/20__

Educate yourself on the practice of restorative justice. Find out about restorative justice efforts in your community.

Day 138 __/__/20__

Find out what states allow the death penalty. Write to or call the governors of those states urging them to rethink such a violent and retributive practice.

Day 139 __/__/20__

Start a conversation with someone you think agrees with you about the rights of those who are incarcerated and the injustice of capital punishment. Generally, work off of the information you've been learning.

Day 140 __/__/20__

Write a short story about imprisonment, being on death row, etc.

**Innocent and guilt lie on a spectrum,
and wherever we find ourselves on that spectrum,
from the most innocent to the most depraved,
nothing can deprive us of our inherent human dignity
and the right to live free from aggressive violence.**

Who you will rehumanize: preborn human beings and their parents

**"When a man steals to satisfy hunger, we may safely conclude that there is something wrong in society – so when a woman destroys the life of her unborn child, it is an evidence that either by education or circumstances she has been greatly wronged."
-Maddie H. Brinckerhoff[50]**

---

[50] Foster, Serrin M. "Women Deserve Better than Abortion: The Ultimate Exploitation of Women." *National Review*, National Review, 19 Jan. 2018, www.nationalreview.com/2018/01/womens-march-pro-life-feminists/.

Day 141 _/_/20_
Look into local peace or pro-life marches coming up. Add them to your calendar and plan to attend.

Day 142 _/_/20_
Do some good stretching before you leave your house for the day. Release the tension from the past week and consider making this a daily habit!

Day 143 _/_/20_
Check your language. Evaluate how the terms you use reflect the truth about preborn human beings, mothers who did not plan on getting pregnant, and more. For example, the term "unborn" gives the impression that the fetus is *not* something, whereas "preborn" shows the the fetus is a living human in the stage before birth. Additionally, it is better to say "fertilization" or "the moment of sperm, egg fusion" than to say "conception", which is not a concrete, medically or scientifically significant term.

Day 144 _/_/20_
Make a sculpture. That's just a suggestion, but you can use any medium of art to express either the violent tragedy of abortion or, contrariwise, the love and care of a parent for their preborn child.

Day 145 _/_/20_
Volunteer at a local adoption agency or charity. You may be able to do something to help from home or you (and maybe a group) could go in to assist with something they need extra hands for.

Who you will rehumanize: human beings victimized by police violence

"Black male offenders continued to receive longer sentences than similarly situated White male offenders," according to a 2017 report on the Demographic Differences in Sentencing done by the U.S. Sentencing Commission.[51]

MappingPoliceViolence.org compiles data on police violence and according to their research, "Police killed 1,147 people in 2017. Black people were 25% of those killed despite being only 13% of the population."

Additionally, of the African Americans killed by police officers (intentionally or not, on or off duty) in 2014 in the U.S., only 31% of them were suspected of a violent crime and allegedly armed.[52]

<u>How has your community been impacted by police brutality?</u>

_____

_____

_____

_____

[51] "Demographic Differences in Sentencing." *United States Sentencing Commission*, 14 Nov. 2017, www.ussc.gov/research/research-reports/demographic-differences-sentencing.

[52] useofforceproject.org. "Police Have Killed 646 People in 2018." *Mapping Police Violence*, mappingpoliceviolence.org/.

Day 146 __/__/20__
Create a sign protesting the injustice of police brutality, bias, and racism. Save it for the next peaceful march or rally to protest police-perpetrated violence near you.

Day 147 __/__/20__
Pose with your handmade sign and post a picture of you with it on social media or in your locker.

Day 148 __/__/20__
Write your local government (city council and mayor, for example) about ensuring that all police departments are trained in the languages of the given region. This includes sign language so they are able to communicate with people who are deaf or hard of hearing.

Day 149 __/__/20__
Find out about local and national laws that fight racism and police brutality. These can be laws already that should be more properly enacted or enforced, or proposed laws which should be lobbied for.

Day 150 __/__/20__
Support a new candidate that cares about this issue. Find out about local, state, and national races and what each candidate plans to do about the issue.

Who you will rehumanize: human beings impacted by unjust wars

Nukes are not Pro-Life!

sign the petition, then join the protest for peace.

www.rehumanizeintl.org/nukes

"There is no hope for the aching world except through the narrow and straight path of nonviolence."
—Mahatma Gandhi[53]

Notes from research and/or reflection:

_____

_____

_____

_____

---

[53] "Application of Non-Violence." *Mind of Mahatma Gandhi: Complete Book Online*, www.mkgandhi.org/momgandhi/chap24.htm.

Day 151 __/__/20__
Find out if your bank is funding war/nuclear weapons. Look into whether they have made investments in any nuclear arms manufacturing companies.

Day 152 __/__/20__
Today, take a bath or a nap to rejuvenate.

Day 153 __/__/20__
Watch a war film and discuss in a group. How were the characters affected by the decisions of others? How well did the movie represent reality?

Day 154 __/__/20__
Write a poem. However you like, express the human rights violations of war through art.

Day 155 __/__/20__
Collect and send donations to those fleeing or enduring violence in a war zone. Look into humanitarian efforts in war torn regions.

Who you will rehumanize: human beings at the embryonic stage of development

The introduction to a webpage on Embryonic Stem Cells, from the National Institutes of Health started like this: "Human embryonic stem (ES) cells capture the imagination because they are immortal and have an almost unlimited developmental potential. After many months of growth in culture dishes, these remarkable cells maintain the ability to form cells ranging from muscle to nerve to blood—potentially any cell type that makes up the body"[54]

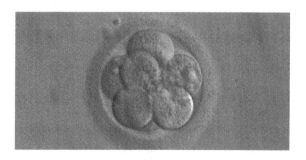

It sounds as though perhaps the NIH is surprised by the fact that developing human beings act exactly as one would expect developing human beings to act: embryonic cells are pluripotent so as to develop into all of the different organs of a fetal human being. They are not pluripotent so that they can be exploited and valuable to researchers.

Embryos are the tiniest of all humans and they need you to stand up and speak for them in their defenseless state!

[54] Thomson, James A, and Junying Yu. "Embryonic Stem Cells." *National Institutes of Health*, U.S. Department of Health and Human Services, stemcells.nih.gov/info/Regenerative_Medicine/2006Chapter1.htm.

Day 156 __/__/20__
Research your own daily-use products: are your cosmetics, food, medicines, or other products made using Embryonic Stem Cells (ESC), whether in development, ingredients, or in testing?

Day 157 __/__/20__
Find out about Rehumanize International's Affiliate Communities. Check out our website to see if there is a community near you in which you could get involved.

Day 158 __/__/20__
Make a collage or other piece of artwork. Embryos are the most unseen class of humans, so make them seen.

Day 159 __/__/20__
Donate to research organizations and projects that work on Adult Stem Cell Research and reject ESCR.
Check out *StemCellResearch.org.*

Day 160 __/__/20__
Choose a movie to watch and discuss with others. I'd recommend "Never Let me Go" to explore the consequences of human cloning and treating humans as means to ends for the use of their body parts.

Did any of your daily-use products use embryonic or fetal stem cells?

_____

_____

_____

Who you will rehumanize: human beings victimized by human trafficking

"Human trafficking is a form of modern slavery—a multi-billion dollar criminal industry that denies freedom to 20.9 million people around the world. And no matter where you live, chances are it's happening nearby. From the girl forced into prostitution at a truck stop, to the man discovered in a restaurant kitchen, stripped of his passport and held against his will. All trafficking victims share one essential experience: the loss of freedom."[55]

Victims of human trafficking are from all economic groups, age groups, races, and sexes. Though traffickers do not discriminate, they do prey especially on vulnerable people such as refugees, immigrants, homeless people, runaway children, and victims of abuse. "Human traffickers recruit, transport, harbor, obtain, and exploit victims – often using force, threats, lies, or other psychological coercion." Once the trafficker has their victim, threats, physical violence, and substance abuse are used to keep control.[56]

Do you know how to recognize signs of trafficking?

_____

_____

_____

_____

---

[55] "Human Trafficking." *Polaris*, 21 Dec. 2017, polarisproject.org/human-trafficking.

[56] "The Victims & Traffickers." *Polaris*, 29 Feb. 2016, polarisproject.org/victims-traffickers.

Day 161 _/_/20_

Start a conversation about human trafficking and modern slavery in America and abroad. Try to bring it up with as many people as you think might not know much about it.

Day 162 _/_/20_

Find out when this year's *Create / Encounter* submission period is. *Create / Encounter* is an annual creative issue of Rehumanize International's *Life Matters Journal.* You've been creating and writing lots of things that relate to the CLE this year through your journey through this book. Plan to submit to *Create / Encounter* at least one thing you've made or been wanting to make.

Day 163 _/_/20_

Buy fair trade products. This means, according to Merriam-Webster, "a movement whose goal is to help producers in developing countries to get a fair price for their products so as to reduce poverty, provide for the ethical treatment of workers and farmers, and promote environmentally sustainable practices".[57] Look for a Fair Trade Certified symbol on your coffee, chocolate, and many more food and clothing purchases.

Day 164 _/_/20_

Literally go to a happy place! Where is someplace you can go to and find a sense of peace and contentment easily? Find a way to get there.

Day 165 _/_/20_

Start to read a fiction or nonfiction book discuss. If you are doing this within the same group each time, make sure everyone gets a chance to choose a book.

---

[57] "Fair-Trade." *Merriam-Webster*, Merriam-Webster, www.merriam-webster.com/dictionary/fair-trade.

Who you will rehumanize: preborn human beings and their parents

A few words on the belief in pro-life feminism, a philosophy many in the mainstream feminist movement would call a contradiction in terms:

On July 19th, 1848 at the Seneca Falls Convention, one of the event's organizers, Elizabeth Cady Stanton drafted a "Declaration of Sentiments, Grievances, and Resolutions." It added only two words to the first sentence of the Declaration of Independence: "we hold these truths to be self-evident: that all men *and women* are created equal." This one sentence embodied and fueled the subsequent women's rights movement for the next 150 years. A little known fact surrounding this popular moment in history: early suffragists such as Stanton, Mott, Susan B. Anthony, and Elizabeth Blackwell were in fact pro-life. They were informed. They pushed back against a male dominated social structure. These women simply rejected the notion that the fight for women's rights requires women to also be at odds with their children.

So, in other words, pro-life feminism is not some new-age distortion of either feminism or the pro-life stance. It is, rather, the most consistent and true form of both philosophies.

As modern human rights activists, we return to the roots of feminist thought and the central principles of feminism: equality, nondiscrimination, and nonviolence.

Day 166 __/__/20__

A pro-choice argument is that there's no point bringing a child into a home that cannot afford to care for them or that it is better that they be aborted than be the child of a drug addict or alcoholic. We know that these are not legitimate reasons to kill another human being, so learn the counter arguments to this. Also check out *drugrehab.com.*

Day 167 __/__/20__

Invite your pro-life friends over to create handmade signs for a march for life. Be sure to photograph (maybe candid this time) and post on social media.

Day 168 __/__/20__

Watch a pro-life movie and discuss. But this time discuss your expectations for the movie before you start it.

Day 169 __/__/20__

Invite a friend or relative to come with you tomorrow to volunteer at a local PRC. Show someone else what a difference they can make.

Day 170 __/__/20__

Volunteer with a PRC. Maybe this time at the Pregnancy Resource Center you can be trained for a new role or responsibility.

Who you will rehumanize: human beings experiencing homelessness

The National Alliance to End Homelessness list these as the causes of homelessness in the U.S.:

- Housing affordability
- Income
- Health
- Domestic violence
- Racial inequality

"Today, 11 million extremely low-income households pay at least half of their income toward housing, putting them at risk of housing instability and homelessness."[58]

Reflection on Day 174's reading:

_____

_____

_____

_____

_____

_____

_____

---

[58] "Housing." *National Alliance to End Homelessness*, endhomelessness.org/homelessness-in-america/what-causes-homelessness/housing/.

Day 171 __/__/20__
Suggest an activity to the Rehumanize Street Team. Contact us over Facebook.

Day 172 __/__/20__
Research and write about the CLE or one of the many issues contained within it. Submit your essay to a local or school newspaper.

Day 173 __/__/20__
Listen to some calming tunes. I tend to go for folk but whatever is soothing for you is best.

Day 174 __/__/20__
Read a short story or personal account from someone who has or is experiencing homelessness. Discuss with others if you like.

Day 175 __/__/20__
Give to charity. You could go through your closet or make a monetary sacrifice and give the unused clothing or money to a nonprofit. Choose one that will give the vast majority of it straight to the needy people in your neighborhood.

Who you will rehumanize: immigrant and refugee human beings

Most Americans do not have to live in poverty. Most of us do not live in fear of gang violence. Most of us have not experienced a war in our homeland. These are some of the factors, often combined into a lethal concoction, that lead people to leave their homes and seek asylum in the United States. Ask yourself how you can effectively rehumanize immigrants and refugees in your own community, family, or group of friends.

What did you get out of your readings and movie this week?:

_____

_____

_____

_____

_____

_____

_____

_____

Day 176 _/_/20_

Read a personal account/short story about or from asylum-seekers and refugees coming from Syria and all of the Middle East.

Day 177 _/_/20_

Watch a movie related to this topic and reflect on it. If you like to write, write a journal entry about it.

Day 178 _/_/20_

Learn about the stories of immigrants and refugees coming from Central America and Mexico. Read personal stories and try to put yourself in their shoes.

Day 179 _/_/20_

Create and/or post flyers for a resettlement organization's services or classes. Post the flyers in public locations near the location of the resettlement agency.

Day 180 _/_/20_

Look into local marches or peaceful protest or vigil for refugee or immigrant rights and dignity. Make plans to attend if you are able.

Who you will rehumanize: elderly human beings and those with terminal illnesses

In addition to the obvious disregard for the dignity of a patient as a human being, PAS undermines the dignity of the doctor. People often become doctors so they can heal other people, but when we ask them to go against that and prescribe potentially lethal medication there are bound to be consequences. The trust between doctors and patients will wear away with time if doctors have the power to kill as well as save. Additionally, assisting in the death of another human being is bound to leave a medical professional with psychological scars, even symptoms of Perpetration Induced Traumatic Stress.[59]

What did you learn this week about the physicians involved in PAS?

_____

_____

_____

_____

_____

_____

_____

_____

---

[59] MacNair, Rachel, and Stephen Zunes. *Consistently Opposing Killing: from Abortion to Assisted Suicide, the Death Penalty, and War.* Authors Choice Press, 2011.

Day 181 __/__/20__
Learn some of the life-affirming arguments against Physician Assisted Suicide (PAS). *http://notdeadyet.org/assisted-suicide-talking-points*

Day 182 __/__/20__
Meet up with a friend and go to the park or the movies. Enjoy life, you only get one.

Day 183 __/__/20__
Find out what efforts in your community or state are working toward a greater respect for the elderly and human beings with terminal illnesses. This can be anything from an activist group lobbying against unjust laws or a community center or charity with a focus on helping give the elderly hope.

Day 184 __/__/20__
Let someone at a nursing home teach you something. In previous visits, if you connected with a particular person or remember someone will a certain skill, see if you can bond over learning it from them. Card games are a fun option.

Day 185 __/__/20__
Make a hat or blanket for babies at the NICU. This could be done with the elderly residents of a nursing home.

Who you will rehumanize: preborn human beings and their parents

Phrases you can chalk on sidewalks:
- Abortion Hurts
- Women Need Love Not Abortion
- Restore Preborn Rights
- Human Rights for All: Born & Preborn
- Human Rights Start When a Human's Life Begins
- Love them Both
- Peace Begins in the Womb
- Pro-choice? That's a lie! Babies never choose to die.
- Equality for Preborn Humans!
- No Violence! No Discrimination! No Abortion!
- End Violence Against Preborn Children
- Equal Rights for Preborn Humans
- Pregnant & Need Help? Visit [local PRC website URL][60]

<u>What are your state's abortion laws?</u>

_____

_____

_____

_____

_____

[60] "Example Messages." *Nationalprolifechalkday.com*, Students for Life of America, www.nationalprolifechalkday.com/example-messages/.

Day 186 _/_/20_

Look at *checkmyclinic.org* to find out about the specific abortion laws in your home state. The website also shows the locations of abortion providing facilities and how they did on their last inspection.

Day 187 _/_/20_

One of the arguments for legalized abortion is that we need it to combat "the overpopulation crisis". Do your own research on this supposed problem (*overpopulationisamyth.com*) and then remember to argue the point of it all: Once a human being exists you cannot kill them.

Day 188 _/_/20_

Read some blog posts from Rehumanize International and post your favorite on social media.
Find them at *https://www.rehumanizeintl.org/blog*

Day 189 _/_/20_

Check back in with the Pregnancy Resource Center (PRC) you've contacted previously or a new one. Create and/or post flyers for their services around the community. Too many people facing unplanned pregnancies feel that abortion is their only option.

Day 190 _/_/20_

Chalk pro-life messaging on the sidewalks at school or another public place. Be clear, uplifting, and maybe include the phone number for a pro-life counseling service, OptionLine, or a PRC. Include friends and get creative... and check the forecast. (If it's raining or about to rain, save this task for another day!)

Who you will rehumanize: human beings impacted by unjust war

"War is the cemetery of futures promised"
-John Cory[61]

---

[61] "Quotes." *Antiwar.com*, www.antiwar.com/quotes.php.

Day 191 __/__/20__

There are many books, fiction and nonfiction, out there about war. When choosing this book be sure it will not glorify war but rather, give an honest look at the consequences soldiers and civilians feel.

Day 192 __/__/20__

Throw a small party or get-together (but don't stress yourself out planning it) or go for a hike. Do something life-affirming that will bring you some happiness.

Day 193 __/__/20__

Go on our website and sign our anti-nuclear weapons petition. *www.rehumanizeintl.org/nukes*

Day 194 __/__/20__

Contact your senator about the military budget. What are your state's representatives prioritizing?

Day 195 __/__/20__

Host a Rehumanize International speaker. Find an audience through your school, church, or other group, then pick a speaker from our website and set up an event.

Who you will rehumanize: human beings experiencing homelessness

"The societal wounds of racism, poverty, and the penchant for using violence to address problems are intimately connected to the death penalty, to war, to the killing of the old and demented, and to the killing of children, unborn and born. If more people were familiar with the consistent life ethic...then the voice of all unseen vulnerable people would be better heard."
-Sister Helen Prejean[62]

In your experiences with nonprofits working to end homelessness, what have you learned? In your interactions with people experiencing homelessness what have you learned?

_____

_____

_____

_____

_____

_____

[62] MacNair, Rachel, and Stephen Zunes. *Consistently Opposing Killing: from Abortion to Assisted Suicide, the Death Penalty, and War.* Authors Choice Press, 2011.

Day 196 _/_/20_

Ask local resource organizations about how you can spread the word about them and their services. Find out how, in general, you can help them succeed in their human-centered efforts.

Day 197 _/_/20_

Watch a movie about a topic within the CLE and discuss with a group or reflect on your own.

Day 198 _/_/20_

Make some thoughtful little cards to give with pocket change to people experiencing homelessness, joblessness, or poverty. Money gets spent quickly, but a word of encouragement is often remembered.

Day 199 _/_/20_

Take one of our downloadable online graphics from the Rehumanize website. Make it your phone background for a while.

Day 200 _/_/20_

Volunteer at a clothing closet or donation center.

Who you will rehumanize: human beings who are or have been incarcerated

"As one whose husband and mother-in-law have died the victims of murder and assassination, I stand firmly and unequivocally opposed to the death penalty for those convicted of capital offenses... An evil deed is not redeemed by an evil deed of retaliation".

-Coretta Scott King (wife of MLK Jr.)[63]

"If we're trying to establish a culture of life, it's difficult to have the state sponsoring executions."

–U.S. Senator Sam Brownback[64]

How did what you learned this week shift your perspective?

_____

_____

_____

_____

_____

---

[63] "Coretta Scott King Quote." *A-Z Quotes*, www.azquotes.com/quote/603069.

[64] MacNair, Rachel, and Stephen Zunes. *Consistently Opposing Killing: from Abortion to Assisted Suicide, the Death Penalty, and War.* Authors Choice Press, 2011.

Day 201 _/_/20_

Today, start a conversation with someone who disagrees with your stance on capital punishment. Be sensitive to the fact that they or a loved one of theirs may have been the victim of a serious crime. After having these sorts of conversations, always reflect on what you learned, could have articulated better, and need to further explore.

Day 202 _/_/20_

Leave yourself a funny voicemail or a nice note.

Day 203 _/_/20_

Look into a current death row case and converse with someone about the case and about the person who was or is being sentenced.

Day 204 _/_/20_

Encourage a friend or family member that lives in a state that has the death penalty to contact their state government about it. You may have to help them see why it is such an injustice and you can help them know what to write or say over the phone.

Day 205 _/_/20_

Reconnect with an inmate you had become pen pals with. You can also review any lessons you learned or stories you heard from you pen pal. Share this experience with people in your life and encourage others to become a pen pal to an inmate.

Who you will rehumanize: preborn human beings and their parents

Many pro-choice people argue that if abortions were made illegal again unsafe abortions would be some people's only choice and society would revert back to the days of women dying from illicit abortions. We know, though, that legal or not, abortion is never safe for the preborn human; not to mention that many women have died from legal abortions since *Roe*.

Roe v. Wade was decided in favor of "choice" based on the premise that it could not be determined when human life begins. Of course, embryology texts would state otherwise. Not to mention, in 1973 when *Roe v. Wade* was decided, ultrasound technology had been in existence for 17 years.[65]

However, even if we couldn't clarify or agree on the exact moment a human life begins, wouldn't it be better to be safe than sorry in a life or death matter? If you procure an abortion without being sure that what is being taken out of your body is human, that wouldn't change what is actually happening. "If a fetus is a person but you don't know that, then abortion is an act of manslaughter. You unintentionally killed an innocent human person."[66] You cannot justify the legality or morality of an action which is shrouded in uncertainty about whether or not the action takes a human life.

---

[65] Lewis, Tanya. "5 Fascinating Facts About Fetal Ultrasounds." *LiveScience*, Purch, 16 May 2013, www.livescience.com/32071-history-of-fetal-ultrasound.html.

[66] "The Uncertainty Principle." *Abort73.Com / Abortion Unfiltered*, 4 Feb. 2017, www.abort73.com/abortion/the_uncertainty_principle/.

Day 206 _/_/20_

We, of course, want to work toward a culture and a system that makes abortion unthinkable and the life-saving alternatives accessible. Learn the talking points to counter the "coat hanger abortions" argument for legalized abortion.

Day 207 _/_/20_

Use a Rehumanize International Facebook profile picture frame. The more opportunities you give for people to strike up conversation with you about the CLE the more you can share the philosophy.

Day 208 _/_/20_

Look into: What is your local government doing to support single and young parents in your community? How can laws be improved to make parenting or the process of making an adoption plan easier options.

Day 209 _/_/20_

Research your state's laws before the 1973 *Roe v. Wade* decision that made abortion legal nationwide. Now, figure out what your state is expected to put into law once Roe has been overturned. Check out *studentsforlife.org/2018/07/25/the-post-roe-safe-zones/* .

Day 210 _/_/20_

Look into Students for Life of America's Pregnant on Campus Initiative. Find a chapter near you and offer your services there or go to the national website and print general flyers. You can post these flyers around your school, community center, library, place of worship, or other places.

Who you will rehumanize: human beings in abusive situations

"You may shoot me with your words,
You may cut me with your eyes,
You may kill me with your hatefulness,
But still, like air, I'll rise."
-Maya Angelou[67]

Here are *a few* warning signs from the National Domestic Violence Hotline website:
- Insults, demeans or shames you with put-downs
- Controls every penny spent in the household
- Shows extreme jealousy of your friends and time spent away
- Prevents you from working or attending school[68]

This is, by far, not an exhaustive list, but gives you an idea.

Reflect on what you'd do if your friend was in an abusive situation:

_____

_____

_____

_____

---

[67] Angelou, Maya. "Still I Rise by Maya Angelou." *Poetry Foundation*, Poetry Foundation, www.poetryfoundation.org/poems/46446/still-i-rise.
[68] "Abuse Defined." *The National Domestic Violence Hotline*, www.thehotline.org/is-this-abuse/abuse-defined/

Day 211 __/__/20__

Learn the warning signs of abuse and always be vigilant in your perceptions of your own relationships and those of others you know.

Day 212 __/__/20__

Rehumanize yourself and have some fun. Get back into an old hobby.

Day 213 __/__/20__

Download our graphics from the Rehumanize International website and share them on social media. If possible pick a topic you have not yet posted about on that media platform.

Day 214 __/__/20__

After contacting a local women's shelter about what donations they need, collect those things and deliver them to the organization. Involve your friends in the collection process. If the shelter does not want donations ask if you can flyer for them, or otherwise help with spreading the word.

Day 215 __/__/20__

Start to read a fiction or nonfiction book and set a date to discuss. If you've been reading on only one topic or from only one genre of book, try to expand beyond that this time.

Who you will rehumanize: human beings with disabilities

In 1997 the disability rights group, Not Dead Yet, protested outside the Supreme Court as it was considering the case of Washington v. Glucksberg. "In wheelchairs and on crutches, and bundled up against the cold the demonstrators held signs that read 'Endangered Species' and 'We are the Target'."[69] The Supreme Court decided unanimously that the right to assisted suicide is not protected by the Due Process Clause.

<u>What ableism did you notice this week? How did you address it?</u>

_____

_____

_____

_____

_____

_____

_____

[69] MacNair, Rachel, and Stephen Zunes. *Consistently Opposing Killing: from Abortion to Assisted Suicide, the Death Penalty, and War.* Authors Choice Press, 2011.

Day 216 _/_/20_

Find out: What is your school/community center is doing about disabilities inclusion? How can you help them improve?

Day 217 _/_/20_

Evaluate the media you consume - whether it tokenizes or holistically includes people with disabilities. The movies, TV shows, books, comics, YouTube channels, etc. you watch and read should all treat people with disabilities with equal respect.

Day 218 _/_/20_

Do something creative for yourself today. The calming effects of doing something artistic are proven!

Day 219 _/_/20_

Using the information you've learned throughout this year, start a conversation about Physician Assisted Suicide with someone. They don't have to agree or disagree with you, just share information with them. Remember that online platforms are not always the best place to discuss important topics like this.

Day 220 _/_/20_

Find out the date and location of a Disability Day of Mourning *(http://disability-memorial.org/)*. This is an annual vigil held in memory of the "victims of filicide – people with disabilities murdered by their family members."[70]

---

[70] "Disability Day of Mourning – Remembering the Disabled Murdered by Caregivers." *Disability Day of Mourning*, disability-memorial.org/.

Who you will rehumanize: human beings victimized by police violence

UseOfForceProject.org "reviewed the use of force policies of America's 100 largest city police departments" examining eight policies within the police departments which restricted the use of force. To varying degrees, "each of the 8 policies examined, police departments that had implemented the policy were less likely to kill people than police departments that had not."

Additionally, they found that putting in place such policies were in the best interest of police officers, because, "officers in police departments with more restrictive policies in place are actually less likely to be killed in the line of duty."[71]

Collect your thoughts here:

_____

_____

_____

_____

_____

_____

_____

_____

---

[71] "Police Use of Force Project." *Police Use of Force Project*, Campaign Zero, useofforceproject.org/#analysis.

Day 221 __/__/20__
Research a local instance of police violence. Be aware, as always, of bias and try to get every side of every story.

Day 222 __/__/20__
Write to your local government (city council and mayor, for example) about use of force standards in your local police department.

Day 223 __/__/20__
Start to a new book! Read a fiction or nonfiction book (on a favorite topic or the CLE generally) and set a date to discuss.

Day 224 __/__/20__
Do something you know relaxes you and affirms your dignity. Maybe it's something you already know, or one of the previous self-care ideas in this book.

Day 225 __/__/20__
Hold or attend a memorial service for victims of police brutality in your region.

How did the event to rehumanize the victims of police brutality go in your community? Did you face backlash? Did you have support? Write your thoughts:

_____

_____

_____

_____

_____

Who you will rehumanize: preborn human beings and their parents

Men have an imperative role to play in the pro-life movement. More men should be encouraged to stand up for the most defenseless of humans and their parents. Ending violence is a human rights issue that everyone can get behind.

Pro-choicers often have signs or bumper stickers saying things like, "No Uterus, No Opinion". Despite the apparent logic in that, it falls short when you realize that anyone willing to fight for human rights, should fight for human rights. Additionally, abortion proponents had no issues with the opinions of the men that made up the entirety of the Supreme Court for the *Roe v. Wade* case.

Pro-life feminists welcome the support of all genders equally. In every human or civil rights movement there are activists fighting for positive change, even though they are not directly or personally impacted by it. However, men do not go unscathed by abortion.[72] Men lose their children to abortion every day, just like women, and in some cases without having any say in what happens to their preborn child. Whether a man was or was not involved in the procurement of an abortion he can feel serious psychological effects. This culture of "take care of it" and "don't involve me," gives men more freedom than ever to use women as means to an end. This is just one of the ways that abortion is a tool of the patriarchy.

---

[72] Snyder, Monica. "'No Uterus, No Opinion.'" *Secular Pro-Life Perspectives*, 1 June 2012, blog.secularprolife.org/2012/06/no-uterus-no-opinion.html.

Day 226 _/_/20_

This week you'll host a pro-life movie screening. Today, select the film for that event. You should choose a movie that you've watched, supports human dignity and human rights, and is enjoyable.

Day 227 _/_/20_

Find an audience through your school, church, or other group. Pick a place, date, time, and start publicizing your event. Will this be a fundraising event for a PRC or other nonprofit? Day 229 has some more things to think about before you go public.

Day 228 _/_/20_

Talk to a birth mom, a person who was adopted, or anyone with a close connection to adoption. See what you can learn from them.

Day 229 _/_/20_

Continuing to plan the movie screening, create discussion questions for after the movies. You can make the discussion a part of the event or an optional add-on. Plan whether your screening will have snacks.

Day 230 _/_/20_

Time to host your movie screening! Get feedback afterward on how to improve for next time.

<u>What have you learned through planning events? What's your take?</u>

_____

_____

_____

_____

_____

Who you will rehumanize: human beings living with mental illness

"Guilt and shame can enter into a toxic battle within an individual that slowly deteriorates their sense of personhood from the core of their being: in other words, from the inside out. It begins as an experience of an all-encompassing, pervasive sense that an individual is flawed and defective as a human being.

Suicide, of any kind, at any age, is a complicated, multi-layered issue, but it is not in the least a hopeless situation. Knowledge of the warning signs of depression and suicidal ideation is key for individuals, families, friends, and communities to be able to recognize it and take action."[73]

<u>What have you learned through conversations and interactions with people with mental illnesses?</u>

_____

_____

_____

_____

_____

_____

---

[73] Jurina, Nicki. "Guilt and Shame versus Unhealthy Blame." *Rehumanize International Blog*, Rehumanize International, 25 May 2016, www.rehumanizeintl.org/single-post/2013/07/02/Guilt-and-Shame-versus-Unhealthy-Blame.

Day 231 _/_/20_

Write for Rehumanize! Share your thoughts on the state of America's mental health care system through a 400 to 1000 word blog post or an article to be published in Life Matters Journal. For more on writing for our journal, check out *www.rehumanizeintl.org/workwithus*.

Day 232 _/_/20_

Do a small act of kindness for a stranger. This sort of thing has been proven to improve the mood of the person doing the act of kindness.

Day 233 _/_/20_

Reach out to a friend that seems down. It's easy to get caught up in your own emotional state, but as everyone around you fights their own battles, so take the time to find out about someone else's struggles.

Day 234 _/_/20_

Talk to someone about their experiences with mental health. Ask friends or family members if they are willing to talk to you about their mental health. If they are receiving help or are otherwise in a better place than previously, see if they have any advice for you or a friend of yours.

Day 235 _/_/20_

Talk to others about starting a Rehumanize Affiliate Community. Look at our website (*https://www.rehumanizeintl.org/community*) for more information on starting your own.

How are *you* feeling this week? Write your thoughts:

_____

_____

_____

Who you will rehumanize: human beings experiencing homelessness

"On a single night in January 2017: 40,056 veterans (approximately 9 percent of all homeless adults) were experiencing homelessness."[74] And an additional "1.4 million veterans are at risk of homelessness."[75]

Veterans, of course, face all the same obstacles to securing affordable housing that other adults do. However, they additionally struggle with the consequences of war-related mental disorders such as anxiety, depression, PTSD, and Traumatic Brain Injury (TBI).

"Be the reason someone smiles. Be the reason someone feels loved and believes in the goodness in people." –Roy T. Bennett[76]

---

[74] "Veterans." *National Alliance to End Homelessness*, endhomelessness.org/homelessness-in-america/who-experiences-homelessness/veterans/.

[75] "2016's Shocking Homelessness Statistics." *Social Solutions*, 9 Jan. 2017, www.socialsolutions.com/blog/2016-homelessness-statistics/.

[76] "A Quote from The Light in the Heart." *Goodreads*, Goodreads, www.goodreads.com/quotes/8110718-be-the-reason-someone-smiles-be-the-reason-someone-feels.

Day 236 __/__/20__

A "blessing bag" as they are sometimes called, is a container of needed items to give to people asking for help on the street. You keep them in your car ready to hand out. A quick google search can give you an idea of what to include and the first person you encounter in need of one might be willing to give you more of an idea. Today, plan what you could include in ones you'll assemble this week. Is there a personal touch you can give them?

Day 237 __/__/20__

Try meditation. There are lots of apps and online resources and books at the library about mindfulness, how to meditate, and its benefits.

Day 238 __/__/20__

Shop for the items to go in your blessing bags.

Day 239 __/__/20__

Put together blessing bags. It's easy to do while chatting on the phone or watching TV. You could include a kind note in each bag.

Day 240 __/__/20__

Find and join a community event. Look into local, one-time volunteer opportunities working to assist the population of people experiencing homelessness.

What did you think about the event?

_____

_____

_____

_____

Who you will rehumanize: human beings with disabilities

From the website of the disability rights group Not Dead Yet:
"Proponents of legal assisted suicide for the terminally ill frequently claim that the opposing views of disability organizations aren't relevant. Nevertheless, although people with disabilities aren't usually terminally ill, the terminally ill are almost always disabled. People with disabilities and chronic conditions live on the front lines of the health care system that serves (and, sadly, often underserves) dying people.

Although intractable pain has been emphasized as the primary reason for enacting assisted suicide laws, the top five reasons Oregon doctors actually report for issuing lethal prescriptions are the "loss of autonomy" (91%), "less able to engage in activities" (89%), "loss of dignity" (81%), "loss of control of bodily functions" (50%) and "feelings of being a burden" (40%).[77] These are disability issues."[78]

<u>Did you know assisted suicide was so ableist? How does that knowledge make you feel?</u>

_____

_____

---

[77] Death with Dignity Act Annual Reports, accessed July 2018.
https://www.oregon.gov/oha/PH/PROVIDERPARTNERRESOURCES/EVALUATIONRESEARCH/DEATHWITHDIGNITYACT/Pages/ar-index.aspx

[78] "Disability Rights Toolkit for Advocacy Against Legalization of Assisted Suicide." *Not Dead Yet*, 1 May 2015,

notdeadyet.org/disability-rights-toolkit-for-advocacy-against-legalization-of-assisted-suicide.

Day 241 __/__/20__
Begin learning sign language to make the world more accessible to people who are deaf and hard-of-hearing. An easy place to start is fingerspelling, which simply uses the ASL alphabet to communicate.

Day 242 __/__/20__
Check your use of wheelchair accessible amenities. Make sure people who really need to use an elevator can get on first and don't use the wheelchair accessible bathroom stall unless necessary.

Day 243 __/__/20__
Think about how you talk to persons with disabilities. Don't ask weirdly personal or insensitive questions like "What happened?" Consider: do you use patronizing or condescending tones when speaking with people with disabilities or talk to them through someone else?[79] If so, change that.

Day 244 __/__/20__
Try a fun new way to exercise. Get some fresh air or join a friend at a class.

Day 245 __/__/20__
Watch a movie and discuss.

What did you think about the movie? Write your thoughts:

_____

_____

_____

---

[79] Tatum, Erin. "10 Ways to Avoid Everyday Ableism." *Everyday Feminism*, 9 Mar. 2014, everydayfeminism.com/2013/10/avoid-everyday-ableism/.

Who you will rehumanize: human beings currently or previously incarcerated

"All states and the federal government use lethal injection as their primary method of execution. States use a variety of protocols using one, two, or three drugs. The three-drug protocol uses an anesthetic or sedative, typically followed by pancuronium bromide to paralyze the inmate and potassium chloride to stop the inmate's heart. The one or two-drug protocols typically use a lethal dose of an anesthetic or sedative."

-Death Penalty Information Center[80]

"People are more than the worst thing they have ever done in their lives"
-Sr. Helen Prejean[81]

---

[80] "Lethal Injection." *Death Penalty Information Center*, deathpenaltyinfo.org/lethal-injection.

[81] "A Quote by Helen Prejean." *Goodreads*, Goodreads, www.goodreads.com/quotes/129660-people-are-more-than-the-worst-thing-they-have-ever.

Day 246 _/_/20_
Sign up for email updates from Rehumanize International to keep up to date on news and all things CLE.

Day 247 _/_/20_
Research how Supreme Court justices feel about capital punishment. What official opinions have they given on previous court cases of their careers?

Day 248 _/_/20_
Follow on social media organizations such as the Death Penalty Information Center, Witness to Innocence, and the Innocence Project.

Day 249 _/_/20_
Give yourself a break. Whatever it is that you have been too hard on yourself about lately, cut it out.

Day 250 _/_/20_
Write an article for Rehumanize blog, *Life Matters Journal*, or a local newspaper about the issue of capital punishment.

Notes for an idea for an article:

_____

_____

_____

_____

_____

Who you will rehumanize: human beings victimized by police violence

America's police use their firearms and kill more people than many other countries such as Germany, Canada, and the UK. There are many ideas out there of what it is that those countries are doing better than us. The Campaign Zero website (*www.joincampaignzero.org*) provides a 10 part solution to the rampant police violence in our country.

- End broken windows policing
- Community oversight
- Limit use of force
- Independently investigate and prosecute
- Community representation
- Body cams/film the police
- Training
- End for-profit policing
- Demilitarization
- Fair police union contracts[82]

Notes on demilitarization of police and nonviolent alternatives:

_____

_____

_____

_____

_____

---

[82] "Solutions." *Campaign Zero*, We The Protesters, www.joincampaignzero.org/solutions/#solutionsoverview.

Day 251 __/__/20__
Educate yourself on the 1033 program that is militarizing the police.

Day 252 __/__/20__
Write your federal representatives about ending the 1033 program.

Day 253 __/__/20__
Research nonviolent alternatives to policing, such as the Project Safe Neighborhood program.

Day 254 __/__/20__
Write your local government (city council and mayor, for example) about ensuring that police live in the area which they will be policing.

Day 255 __/__/20__
Attend a social justice training in your area. Check out your local YWCA or other human rights groups for opportunities.

What did you like about nonviolent alternatives to policing?

_____

_____

_____

_____

_____

_____

_____

_____

Create your own week of social justice.

Who you will rehumanize:

_____

_____

_____

_____

_____

_____

_____

"Where life is involved, the service of charity must be profoundly consistent. It cannot tolerate bias and discrimination, for human life is sacred and inviolable at every stage and in every situation; it is an indivisible good.
We need then to show care for all life and for the life of everyone".
- Pope John Paul in 1995[83]

---

[83] Paul, John. "Evangelium Vitae (25 March 1995) | John Paul II." *Vatican*, Libreria Editrice Vaticana, w2.vatican.va/content/john-paul-ii/en/encyclicals/documents/hf_jp-ii_enc_25031995_evangelium-vitae.html.

Day 256 _/_/20_

_____

_____

Day 257 _/_/20_

_____

_____

Day 258 _/_/20_

_____

_____

Day 259 _/_/20_

_____

_____

Day 260 _/_/20_

_____

_____

You did it!

Honestly, you should be proud of you. Sticking through the challenges for a whole year is mighty impressive! You have passion, you have dedication, you have demonstrated that you can live a consistent life.

How do you think this year changed you? What is the most important thing you have learned? What was the activity that impacted you the most? Write your reflections below.

_____

_____

_____

_____

_____

_____

_____

_____

_____

_____

_____

_____

Keep up the good work!

This is the end of this book,
but just the beginning of *your* activism story.

Index

Resource List

These stories do not all have morals to them that align with the CLE, but they do offer a compelling launch pad for reflection and discourse.

<u>Books and Short Stories:</u>

1. *One Dress One Year* by Susanna Foth Aughtmon (human trafficking)
2. *Slaughterhouse 5* by Kurt Vonnegut (war, sci-fi)
3. *Cat's Cradle* by Kurt Vonnegut (nuclear warfare, sci-fi)
4. *Consistently Opposing Killing* edited by Stephen Zunes, Rachel MacNair (Consistent Life Ethic)
5. *Inside America's Concentration Camps* by James Dickerson (war, racism, torture, history)
6. *Human Embryos, Human Beings* by Maureen L. Condic and Samuel B. Condic (embryology, abortion, ESCR)
7. The Ones Who Walk Away From Omelas by Ursula K. Le Guin (dystopian, philosophy, the value of a single human life)
8. *A Canticle for Leibowitz* by Walter M. Miller Jr. (post-apocalyptic, sci-fi)
9. *1984* by George Orwell (dystopian, political fiction)
10. *Ender's Game* and *Speaker for the Dead* by Orson Scott Card (sci-fi, dystopian)
11. *Brave New World* by Aldous Huxley (dystopian, genetic modification)
12. *My Sister's Keeper* by Jodi Picoult ("designer babies", "savior siblings," consequentialism, suicide, and medical ethics)
13. *Armageddon in Retrospect* by Kurt Vonnegut (war)
14. *Braving the Wilderness: The Quest for True Belonging and the Courage to Stand Alone* by Brené Brown (community, rehumanization)
15. Harrison Bergeron by Kurt Vonnegut (dystopian, sci-fi, human dignity and selfhood)
16. *Eight O'Clock Ferry to the Windward Side* by Clive Stafford Smith (nonfiction, Guantanamo Bay)

Resource List, continued

Movies and TV shows:

1. Fatal Flaws - *from the Euthanasia Prevention Coalition*
2. Sophie Scholl: The Final Days - *WWII, nonviolent resistance*
3. Band of Brothers - *war miniseries that doesn't glorify war (very gory)*
4. Children of Men - *sci-fi, drama, infertility, the value of a child*
5. Arrival - *sci-fi, drama, war, diplomacy, choosing life*
6. Minority Report - *drama, fantasy, criminal justice*
7. Never Let Me Go - *drama, dystopian, medical ethics, cloning*
8. Shawshank Redemption - *prisons, justice, human dignity*
9. Hunchback of Notre Dame - *racism, general pro-life themes*
10. My Sister's Keeper - *"designer babies", medical/legal ethics*
11. Dollhouse - *TV show, sci-fi, dehumanization, human traffick*
12. Me Before You - *disability, assisted suicide, euthanasia (not a pro-life film, but good for discourse)*
13. A Beautiful Mind - *mental illness, human dignity*
14. Wonder - *disabilities, kindness, human dignity*
15. Gattaca - *sci-fi, dystopian, "designer babies", embryos*
16. Bella - *abortion, the dignity of prisoners*
17. The Bucket List - *drama, end of life, terminal illness*
18. Big Fish - *drama, illness, end of life, human dignity*
19. Taxi to the Dark Side - *documentary, torture, Bush admin*
20. Ghosts of Abu Ghraib - *documentary, torture, Iraq's Abu Ghraib prison*
21. HUSH - *documentary, abortion, breast cancer, mental health*
22. Pro-Life Feminist - *short documentary, interviews 3 movement leaders, including Aimee Murphy the founder of Rehumanize International*

About Rehumanize International

Rehumanize International is a non-profit human rights organization
dedicated to creating a culture of peace and life
and in so doing, we seek to bring an end to all aggressive violence
against humanity
through education, discourse, and action.
We want to ensure that each and every human being's life is
respected, valued, and protected.

As such, we oppose all forms of aggressive violence, including but not
limited to:
abortion
unjust war
capital punishment
euthanasia
torture
embryonic stem cell research
assisted suicide
abuse
human trafficking
police brutality
etc...

Additionally, we will achieve our vision by maintaining our organization
as non-sectarian, and non-partisan, and furthermore by promoting
collaboration amongst many organizations across movements.

About the Authors

Mary Grace Coltharp

Mary Grace Coltharp served as an intern for Rehumanize International during the summer of 2018. She was awarded the Y.E.S. (Youth Exemplifying Service) Award for her volunteer work at a church and with a community in Tamara, Honduras during one of her summer breaks. After graduating high school, she went on to take a gap year dedicated to service of her fellow human beings. Travelling not only the country but also the globe, she served all people, from the preborn and their parents in Texas to the poor elderly in NYC. She strives to bring her passion for human dignity into every sphere of her life.

She currently attends Mount St. Mary's University in Emmitsburg, MD and is searching for the major that will lead her to make a meaningful impact on the world.

Aimee C. Murphy

Aimee Murphy is the founder and Executive Director of Rehumanize International, a non-partisan, secular organization dedicated to bringing an end to all aggressive violence against human beings through education, discourse, and action. After a personal conversion to the cause against abortion as a teen, she was able to identify and defend a holistic ethic of non-violence during her time in university: the Consistent Life Ethic. Through her work with Rehumanize International, Aimee is reaching people all over the globe with the consistent message of human rights and is creating and engaging in effective dialogue to change hearts and minds.

Aimee currently resides in Pittsburgh with her profoundly supportive husband Kyle, their dog, and --in the spirit of radical hospitality-- whichever friends wander into the Murphy household.

Made in the USA
Middletown, DE
19 December 2020